learning rhythm

an afro-folktale

kwabena foli

in memory of

Shawna Clahar Williamson
(1975 - 2015)

who introduced me to the
magic of friendship, honesty
and being unapologetically
afrikan.

i suck at writing
poems but not at being
honest with myself.

do duh work.

- Baba Kwesi (1960-2016)

sun. [blk man]

ocean. [blk womyn]

eclipse. [fuckboy]

tempest. [her]

the great balance.

author notes:

1. an afro-folktale is my own take of a biomythography -
    a cultural method of writing coined by Audre Lorde for
    self exploration and truth-sharing.

2. content was created from three years of journaling.

3. i recommend a journal to record & process your own
    experiences as you have them.

a blk man's heart
is a fiery furnace

a place where G-d walks
freely
just to tell the world

i ain't phased by ya smoke.

i am an ocean
all i know
is how to be still
or consume
everything.

what is love?

    tell me
    would you walk up to a flower
    and ask "who are you?"

of course not you just
enjoy it.

    exactly.

- breathe it in

whatever style hides my fears
is what i will
become.

- cool pose

swallowing truth
rather than speaking it
is
an
act of violence
towards
yourself.

i don't know how to let go
without destroying the world around me
and when i do
only an ocean
can stop the bleeding.

blk man. you are more
than a dormant volcano.

negus will never chill
while caged.

- why we must get free

do yourself a favor.

be a gift.

open yourself up.

and enjoy what you find.

they say
if you play with fire
you'll get burned

but who ever said
loving yourself
would be easy.

i love blk men.

    translation:

i love the image of G-d.

    translation:

i love myself.

don't forget

creation and all it's glory

felt empty to man

until Eve came into the picture.

some womyn
have too much magic in their fingers
to even write a name
without conjuring
a wooing.

sunday afternoon nap.

everything from
the brim of my nose
to the cuff of my chin
was buried in her fro.
the aroma
reminded me of a time
when i was G-d in another life
resting on the seventh day
because on the sixth

she appeared

and upon seeing my reflection
in her eyes
i knew

rest.

mystery
draws me in.
possibilities
make me stay.

theory does not suffice.
you have to ride it
to know what it's like.

you make a blk man blush.

"she's a goddess" is an insult.
god has no gender.
just pure spirit.
she's pure.
she's spirit.
she's all god.
god is all she.

please.
no more poems.
or quotes.
or hashtags.
on how much my skin deserves reverence.
put your body where your mouth is.
talk is cheap.
and change
is too expensive
for words.

#blacklivesmatter

heal thyself.

the one command
if everyone followed
would make tragic days
more fiction
than autobiography.

i've always
had a hard time
following directions.

tell me to sink and i'll fly.
tell me to hide and i'll glow.
tell me to hate
and i'll break open my chest
to let love pour out
like a spilled secret.

your love speaks a gospel to me.

anything worth holding onto
requires getting dirty and deep
to find. like

pearls.
diamonds.
gold.

so never apologize for being
difficult to love
for no one loves a treasure
they didn't have to work for.

her eyes
and gestures
rumbled me like thunder
across the sky.

she then said

don't cum for me
'less i sin for you.

- genesis

you can never hurt me so much
that i won't look in your eyes
and still feel
you are the universe's
greatest gift
to me.

how did you know?

i was comfortable with the silence
between us. for desire is not always loud
and most of what needs to be known
doesn't come from the lips.

she told me
the way i fucked
reminds her of thunder.

the rumblings
makes her feel holy.
loves the sermons
the sky preaches. that

no matter how bossy
she becomes
or how high she climbs
the corporate ladder
everything around her
is pending ash
and she too will return to dust.

so she loves to be
undone
as if my body
was a flash in the sky
and she
was the world

ready to burn.

when alone - eyes closed
i hear everything
G-d has been trying to say.

with you - eyes closed
i experience everything
G-d has been wanting me to feel.

do not use fire
as a metaphor
for my vagina

    she tells me.

use water.

    why
    i asked.

because water brings
life to everything
and you was dead before
you met me.

i love it when she is on top.
just as she loves pleasing
a man
who knows his place.

dear music.

when love is a dry spell.
rain on me.

- 90's R&B

a wing and a prayer
is how my grandmother got through.

tending to my body
as a temple
is how i will honor her labor
and stay free.

a headache while you're sitting on the red line towards
Howard which is a 45 minute ride from where you are and
there is no reception on the train so you can't make up
the work you didn't do for school because you've spent the
day high watching 90's movies while rubbing on her booty
and now the light hurts your eyes and your heart pounds
a little heavier because you've also blown all your money
including yesterday's forty-dollar salmon plates now
bills are due and rent is approaching and you have no
steady income because instead of using your degree you
decided to be a poet and you can't tell if it's because of
the womyn you hate to care for or the many other things
in your life either delayed or no more which makes you
want to skip death and just be reincarnated as a new man
but none of that even matters anyway because when you
are both together and your skin touches her's everything
feels like a do-over.

- love | fast

today
another blk boy
died. another blk boy's
blood knows the
taste of concrete.

one america will
weep for these boys.
while the other
praises god
for the new strand of red
weaved into the flag.

when i set fire
to the stars and stripes
i am not being unpatriotic.
i just miss the blk boys

so much.

that i attempt
a resurrection.

black lives matter.
       kids matter.
       minds matter.
       feelings matter.
       bodies matter.
       lands matter.
       histories matter.
       trans matters.
       love matters.
       arts matter.
       scholars matter.
       churches matter.
       Jesus matters.
       music matters.
       hair matters.
       schools matter.
       families matter.
       futures matter.

yelling is how i cry.

```
me:    i feel
       my blk skin
       is a target
       wherever i go.

G-d:   no worries.
       the world could
       never handle
       me either.
```

foreign fire and bang.
wooden sea monsters.
thunder whips.
iron chains.
Jim's crow.
Edgar's Hoover.
Katrina's levee's.
Donald's Trumpet.

blk don't crack
was a phrase way before
it was a compliment
to our skin.

blk boy be winning.
blk boy be fly.
blk boy did everything right.
blk boy suddenly dies.
blk boys see this cycle.
day by day in their lives.
so when blk boys are yelled at to be better.
blk boys think.

why?

today i am profoundly sad
and impulsive.
these are constant strongholds
i contend with.
if either one defeats me
call me a blk man who won
trying to get to the other side
of what was killing him.

- september 5th, 2015

i am blk and human
borrowing strength from prayers.

i am blk and human
borrowing my strength

as all people do.

i'm beginning
to compare myself to others
again.

soon
i'll be a nightmare.

again.

as a blk man
i sometimes wonder
who will kill me first.

my government.
my community.
myself.

blk men were made
as gods

it was the world
that turned them
into ordinary.

sometimes
while riding the train
i catch myself
frozen.
and barely breathing.

being a blk man in america
i guess

this practice is instinctual.

be a flower.

still
growing
using what Jah provides.
this is what makes you beautiful.
this is how we rise.

be a flower.

what is growth?

...not dying.

we cannot hate
hate
out of this world.

- fuck the system

i know hate is wrong
but it is the only emotion with the fuel
to get me through the other side
of crying.

help
is for the strong too.

- when asked about your needs

i am a blk man
screaming for help in a world
where my voice is mistaken
for gunshots.

The problem is not smarter than you.

The problem is not tougher than you.

The problem invokes fear.

The problem is relentless.

The problem is savage.

The problem will not survive you.

sometimes you gotta feel through the sadness.

- today

i am still angry about Mike Brown
just because i haven't tweeted about it
doesn't mean i've stopped
wishing for every blk mother's tear
to purge this world
with no ark
to rescue.

doing something in the name
of faith

is not the same

as doing something
with faith.

one battle at a time.

- focus

everyday

i feel like i'm losing
my mind
only to find it
right there
where my heart was.

i am
not
there
when she reaches for me.
she cries
for loving another blk man
who
is
a
ghost.

- haunted

if you want to die slowly

lie about the love in your life
that's changing you.

every
boy
has hid underneath a blanket
from his fears.

tragically

they grow up
replacing the blanket
for wombs.

- fuckboys

i will never
be your secret.
i am gospel.
proclaim me
from the rooftops.

to love
is
to
suffer.

       then i will keep
       my heart
       to myself.

that's unfortunate
because to love
is also
to
live.

what i need is air.

- space

this is the moment
where love really matters.
after this hurt.
after this pain.
where i must decide
if i want you back
or
if i want you dead.

leave
so i can find the god
i lost within myself
while i was
worshipping you.

stop saving me
with your tongue
after we fight.

hearing my moans
and hearing my heart

are two different things.

you are a bounced check.

i'm tired
of making something
out of nothing
with you.

love binds everything together.
that's why when i started
falling apart
i knew
you
were a lie.

life is about growing up
while learning to accept yourself.

- something heard in prayer

when the surface beneath you
moves as your emotions do
you'll cling to whomever
is
close
like a lifeline.

get ya shit together
or
forever be haunted
by what the best version
of yourself
would've been like.

i've caused more tears than smiles.
more bad nights than good mornings.

you may say: he is a blk man. still
                  repeating generational
                  curses.

others may say: he is a human. doing
                  the best he can.

truth is: i am between the two.

my bones remember you

then ache.

i will not hold onto the past
but let the future embrace me
as my heart
learns
to
heal.

my head is a funhouse of mirrors.
never showing the true image of me.
it's not fun
nor a house.
but a prison in me.

i can't shatter an image
without shattering me.
to be whole
must be broken.

piece
by
piece.

the past is not the mirror
but the frame
it can only set the stage
for your reflection
but you determine
who stares back at you.

how are you doing?

    i'm falling apart.

then why aren't you
showing it?

    because every part
    is falling into the right
    place.

what does blk magic
taste like.

            forgiveness
            and honey.

real life fairy tales
are the kind where you learn
to be the answer
to your own prayers.

funny

i used to be terrified of death
'till i was introduced to love
nobody told me
they grew up together
as twins.

you don't need to get the darkness out.
you just need to let the light
in.

feed yourself.

- light

da hell is happening?
this is unfair.
i hate myself.
i need help.
i'm nobody.
broken into.
broken in two.
but i am magic.
i must be magic.
to still live.
to still love.
a miracle.
i must be.
i am love.
i am loved.
still healing.
ever healing.
but soon
and now
free.

- orgasm

G-d is in the room right now.
if you do not see

look closely in the mirror.

those
that don't know my story
look at me today
as someone covered in dirt
but i know
who i really am.

the ground cracked open
and swallowed me whole
but i refused to die.
i was violent and wild
until the earth spewed
me out of its mouth.

i told life

        take your best shot.
        it'll only make me
        stronger.

then i got hit
right in the heart.
so i asked life

        what's the deal
        i thought i'll be stronger
        now all i feel
        is weak.

life responded

        no
        you just feel more human
        and that's all the strength
        you've ever needed.

i see clearly
only a few days out the year.

most days are fog.

but when i do see
i know i'm heading
down
the
right
path.

shame has a way of
distorting reality
by using a little bit of truth
mixed
with a whole bunch of lies.

yes
you screwed up
but you are no screw-up.

you are a phoenix
who got smothered in its own ashes
while trying to learn
how to fly again.

keep slaying
for there are two kinds of people.

those who criticize.
and those
who give the world something
to critique.

nothing ever ends

except the old you.

accept the new you.

and celebrate

when that person ends

too.

love yourself.

it is revolution.

the only kind.

the world ever needs.

epilogue.

how did you know
that you were meant
to be a healer?

     because i kept
     falling in love
     with broken people.

then why
are you alone?

     because i'm broken too.
     so i am falling
     in love with myself
     to get a taste
     of my own medicine.

to be continued...

kwabena foli was born in Belgium and raised in the
Southside of Chicago. He is a former Chicago poetry slam
champion and national poetry slam finalist. His content
has appeared on platforms such as All Def Poetry and is
included in the anthology Revise the Psalm: Work
Celebrating the Writing of Gwendolyn Brooks. He is
currently a teaching artist in New York City.

Made in the USA
Columbia, SC
16 September 2017